Made in the USA
Columbia, SC
30 January 2022

55068693R00061